KEYS AND DREAMS
GRADE BY GRADE

BY
VASILIKI DIMAKOPOULOU

DEDICATION

To Ioanna, Anastasios and Filippos my three brightest notes in the symphony of life

INTRODUCTION

Learning the piano is more than playing the right notes at the right time. It is about expression, imagination, and discovering the stories that music can tell. Every phrase can paint a picture, every rhythm can set a scene, and every melody can carry an emotion.

This book pairs each piece in the Trinity syllabus with a short story designed to reflect its character. The stories guide pupils to hear the music in new ways, helping them connect emotionally with what they play while finding fresh motivation to practice.

For teachers, it offers a practical tool to make lessons more engaging.

For parents, it provides a creative way to support learning at home.

For pupils, it transforms practice into an adventure one where the piano becomes a doorway to other worlds.

Behind every piece lies a universe waiting to be discovered. This book is an invitation to step inside.

ACKNOWLEDGEMENTS

The Keys and Grades is dedicated to all my pupils, who have been my greatest inspiration. Their curiosity, imagination, and love for music encouraged me to bring these stories to life. Without them, these books would never have been completed.

I would like to thank my daughter, Ioanna, whose constant encouragement gave me strength throughout this journey. I am also deeply grateful to my dear friends Mavra, Mary, and Matoula, who continuously nurtured my confidence and reminded me to believe in myself.

A special thank you goes to my tutor, Lucinda Mackworth Young, whose guidance shaped my teaching, and to the PTC tutors especially Sally Cathcart who taught me how to become a better piano teacher and how to weave stories into music lessons. Their wisdom has been invaluable.

My heartfelt thanks also go to my publishers, Harry, Alisha, and especially Ethan from Publishers House. Without their support, expertise, and belief in this project, none of this would have been possible.

Last but not least, to my best advisor and companion during this journey, Apollon whose insight and constant presence made the process not only possible, but joyful.

"This book is for all who believe in the magic of music and stories."

TABLE OF CONTENT

Turkish March	09
Wild Mignonette	13
Little Stream	17
Morning	21
Mountain Spirit	25
Harry and Ginny	29
Once Upon a December	33
Angry Birds	37
Dynamite (BTS)	41
Chord Etude	45
All Blues or "Blue Notes at Midnight"	49
Tres Palabras	53

GRADE 3

Turkish March

By Gustav Cornelius Gurlitt
1820-1901

There was once a leader in a great nation — a country where the wind smelled of spices, the mountains touched the sky, and history echoed through stone and sand.

He was strong. Wise. Respected.

And for many years, his country had marched.

Marched in battle.
Marched in war.
Marched to the sound of drums and orders and flags waving in the wind.

But one morning, the leader stood before his generals and said something no one expected:

"From this day on, we will not train soldiers for war.
We will train musicians for peace."

The generals blinked.

"But sir," they said, "how will we defend our land?"

The leader smiled.

"With music.
With harmony.
With rhythm that reaches the hearts of our enemies before our weapons ever could."

He gathered people from every corner of his country — not to fight, but to play.
- Flute players marched beside drummers.
- Trumpets replaced rifles.
- Banners were painted with musical notes instead of symbols of war.

Even the youngest children joined, clapping tambourines and singing folk melodies passed down from their grandparents.

And so began the March for Peace.

They didn't conquer countries —
they visited cities, mountains, and villages with concert parades.

They didn't invade borders —
they crossed them with friendship and song.

And every time they played the march — proud, rhythmic, joyful — the people didn't run or hide.

They danced.

Even the wind seemed to join in, whistling between the flutes and tapping through the drums.

Years passed.

Other countries began to copy them — building armies of music, not weapons.

It became a tradition: whenever two nations were on the verge of conflict, they would each send musicians instead of soldiers.

They would meet in the middle.

And play.

Not to win.
Not to fight.
But to listen.

Because a march can still be strong...
A march can still be proud...
But when it is played in duet —
it becomes something even greater:

A march for peace.

Let's explore music

Rhythm & March Character

1. What makes this piece sound like a march?
   Is it the rhythm? The tempo? The regular beat?
2. Can you feel the "steps" in the music?
   Which hand or part sounds like the feet of a marching parade?
3. Is the rhythm strict and steady or playful and light?
   How can you show that in your playing?
4. If this were a real parade for peace, how would you walk to the music?
   (Strong and proud? Gentle and joyful?)

Articulation & Emotion

5. What kind of articulation do you hear?
   (Staccato? Accents? Legato?)
   How does this affect the character of the music?
6. Do any sections sound more serious or more joyful?
   What emotions do you think the musicians in the story might express?
7. Where could you add a sense of "celebration" or "hope" into the duet?
   How can both players help express that?
8. If the music had lyrics, what kind of message would they carry?
   Try writing a short line that could be sung with the melody.

Duet & Dialogue

9. How do the two parts (Primo and Secondo) work together?
   Are they equal partners?
   Does one lead while the other supports?
10. What happens if one player goes too fast or too loud?
    What does this teach us about peace and listening?
11. Can you think of this duet as a conversation between two countries?
    What are they saying to each other?
12. How does playing in a duet feel different from playing solo?
    How does this connect to the story's message about harmony and peace?

Wild Mignonette
by Gustav Cornelius Gurlitt
1820-1901

Germany, 1917.
In a quiet village surrounded by forest and fields, a boy named **Matthias** lived with his mother and two younger brothers.

He was 14 years old.

The war had taken many fathers from the village, including his own.

His father was a soldier at the front.
Letters were rare. Hope was quiet. And days passed slowly.

But there was one place where Matthias felt peaceful:
The garden behind their cottage.

There, he cared for the vegetables, watched bees tumble over clover, and studied the **wild mignonette** — a soft yellow flower with a scent like sunlight after rain.

It was his favourite.

He spoke to it every morning while watering the soil:

"Please… tell the sky to send him back."

He didn't shout. He didn't cry.
He painted.

Matthias had learned from his father, who used to sketch flowers on old scraps of newspaper before the war. Now, Matthias tried to capture the exact curve of the wild mignonette's stem, the tiny details of each bloom, the golden color that seemed to hum in the sunlight.

He painted **every day**.

And as winter turned into spring, and the mignonette began to bloom again, Matthias finished his painting — soft yellows, pale greens, a blue sky in the corner.

He set down his brush. The light came through the window.

And then — a knock.

His mother ran to the door.

Matthias stayed frozen by the window.

He heard her cry out.

And then… footsteps.

A shadow.

And then arms around him.

His father.

Thin, tired, dusty with travel — but alive.

The war was over.

And the mignonette was blooming.

That night, his father looked at the painting and said:

"This… is peace. You saw it even when the world didn't."

Years later, Matthias became a painter. Not of battles, not of kings — but of gardens, flowers, and hope.

And every year, he returned to that same patch of earth, where the wild mignonette still bloomed — quietly, faithfully.

And in every painting, there was a little yellow flower…
a silent promise that peace always finds its way home.

Let's explore music

Mood & Imagery

1. What kind of mood does the music create?
   (Calm? Sad? Hopeful? Gentle?)
   How does it match the garden or the feeling of waiting?
2. Can you imagine the wild mignonette flower while listening or playing?
   What colors, shapes, or smells come to mind?
3. Which part of the music feels like the moment Matthias finishes his painting?
   How can you show that with your dynamics and phrasing?
4. If this piece had a season, which one would it be — spring, summer, autumn, or winter? Why?

Expression & Tone

5. Is the melody mostly smooth (legato) or broken (staccato)?
   How does that affect the feeling of the piece?
6. Where does the music breathe — where do you hear a pause or a sigh?
   Could that be like the moment when Matthias talks to the flowers?
7. What kind of dynamics are used in this piece (louds/softs)?
   Where would you play more quietly — and why?
8. Can you imagine this melody as a voice?
   Is it singing, whispering, telling a secret, or calling out?

Little Stream
by Irona Jurnickova
1947-

Prague, 1955.
The air was cool and smelled of coal smoke and river mist.

The war had ended ten years earlier, but life in Prague was still quiet, careful.
Families lived simply. Streets were clean but faded. And the old trams rattled past the Vltava River like tired songs.

But one place still sparkled:
The National Opera House.

Every evening, golden light spilled from its windows.
Men in hats. Women in fur-lined coats. The sound of orchestras rising from within.
Outside the great building, on a little stone corner by the river, stood a girl named **Eliska**.

She was 14 years old.
She wore worn shoes and a wool coat two sizes too big.
In her hands: a basket of flowers.

"Roses! Carnations! One crown each!"

She sold them with a bright smile. Not because she loved selling flowers — but because it let her stand close enough to hear the music echoing from the marble walls.

Eliska had never seen the inside of the opera house.
But she had a secret:

She knew all the songs.

Every night, after the crowds had gone in and her basket was nearly empty, Eliska would walk to the stone railing above the Vltava.

She'd toss her unsold flowers into the water one by one,
and she would **sing**.

Not loudly — just enough for the water to carry the notes downstream.

She sang arias from Carmen, Aida, and La Boheme, copying them from old records she listened to at the local library.

"One day," she whispered,
"I will be the one they come to see."

And one night... someone did.

As Eliska was singing softly into the wind, a woman in a black coat passed along the riverside.

She stopped.
Listened.
Waited until the final note faded like a petal on the water.

"Who taught you to sing like that?" the woman asked.

Eliska froze. "No one," she said. "I... I just listen."

The woman stepped into the light.
It was the soprano — the star of the National Opera.

"Then let me teach you," she said.

Years later, Eliska stood on that same stage — inside the opera house, not outside.

She wore velvet and lace. The chandeliers shimmered above her.
And the orchestra began the overture to Carmen.

In the front row, her old flower basket sat on an empty chair — filled now with red roses.

And far below, the Vltava flowed quietly... carrying her dream forward, like a little stream that never stopped moving.

Because sometimes, even the quietest dream... finds its way to the stage.

Let's explore music

Mood & Expression

1. What is the mood of this piece?
   (Gentle? Dreamy? Hopeful? Sad?)
2. Can you imagine the little stream while listening or playing?
   What does it look and sound like — smooth, bubbling, fast, calm?
3. Which part of the piece feels like Eliska is singing to the river?
   How would you shape that melody differently?
4. Are there any moments in the music that feel like a pause, like Eliska watching the flowers float away?
   How would you reflect that in your playing?
8. Can you imagine this melody as a voice?
   Is it singing, whispering, telling a secret, or calling out?

Melody, Phrasing & Technique

5. Is the melody mostly legato (smooth) or staccato (detached)?
   How does this affect the way the music flows?
6. Can you find a phrase that rises and then falls, like the river or like a voice singing?
   Where would you breathe or lift your hands slightly?
7. Does the left hand feel like an accompaniment or part of the flowing water?
   How can you make it sound soft but supportive?
8. Do any notes feel especially emotional or important — like a "spotlight" in the melody?
   How can you highlight them gently?

Morning
by Alanya Bridge
1984-

Most people, when they hear the word "morning," imagine things like sunshine, birdsong, butterflies, and golden clouds.

But this is not that kind of story.

This story is about an 8-year-old vampire named Vladko.

Yes, that kind of vampire — fangs, cape, castle in Transylvania. But Vladko wasn't quite like the rest of his family.

While the other vampires slept in their cold stone coffins, dreaming of bats and shadows and garlic-free dinners, Vladko tiptoed outside.

He loved the morning.

He loved the way the sunlight warmed the castle garden, the way the mist curled over the hills, and how squirrels did little acrobatic tricks between the branches.

Most of all, he loved chasing butterflies — not to catch them, just to laugh when they escaped.

He didn't drink blood (bleh!). He liked chamomile tea and vanilla ice cream.

He didn't play organ music in the dark. He hummed tunes that sounded like birds waking up.

And he didn't want to go to the creepy Night School for Young Vampires, where they learned Advanced Hissing and Dramatic Cape-Swooshing.

He wanted to go to Morning School.
With regular kids.
With lunchboxes.
And sunlight.

One day, Vladko sat down with his father — Count Velimir the Very Grumpy.

"Father," Vladko said, "I need to tell you something."

"Go on, my son," said the Count, sipping his tomato juice.

"I… I don't want to be a night vampire. I want to be a morning vampire. I want to play in the light. And I want to go to regular school."

There was silence.

The Count blinked once.
Then twice.

"You… want to go where the sun is?!"

"Yes," said Vladko bravely. "I think I was born for the morning."

The Count was speechless. The bat hanging on the chandelier fainted.

But after a long pause, something even stranger happened…

The Count smiled.

"Well, I never liked hissing practice either," he said quietly.

So the next week, Vladko went to Morning School. At first, it was hard. The other kids didn't understand why he wore a cape, had fangs, or flinched near garlic bread.

But slowly… they began to like him.

He was polite. He shared his snacks (mostly).
And he told the funniest stories about moonlight pillow fights and shadow puppets in dungeons.

And every morning, when the music teacher played a gentle piece on the piano, Vladko would sigh and say:

"This… is what home feels like."

Some people are born for the night.
Some are born for the morning.
And some — like Vladko — are born to remind us it's okay to be different.

Let's explore music

Mood & Imagery

1. What kind of morning does this piece sound like?
   Is it a calm sunrise? A playful morning in a garden? Or something more magical?

2. If this music were the weather, what would it be?
   (Clear and sunny? Cool and misty? Breezy with light clouds?)

3. What part of the story matches this piece best?
   Vladko sneaking out into the garden?
   Chasing butterflies?
   Telling his father the truth?

4. Can you picture the sunlight in the music?
   Which parts feel "bright," and how do the notes make you feel that?

Expression & Phrasing

5. Is the melody mostly smooth (legato) or light and bouncy (staccato)?
   How would you describe how it moves — floating, skipping, or gliding?

6. Where are the phrases in the music?
   Can you show them with breath-like shaping (as if Vladko were humming)?

7. Which dynamics (loud/soft) show a change in mood?
   Where does the music feel like a secret, and where does it feel open?

8. How can you make the piece sound gentle and warm — like morning sunlight?

Mountain Spirit
by Mari Sainio
1989-

Northern Finland. Winter.
The snow covered everything — trees, roads, even the lakes.
It made the world silent.
So silent, you could hear your own thoughts.

And in the distance, rising like a giant frozen wave, stood Korvenvaara — the mountain the villagers called "The Keeper."

It was said to be guarded by a spirit — not a ghost, not an animal, not a person.
Something older than language.
A presence in the snow and wind, watching, listening.

Most people didn't believe it.
But Aleksi and his little sister Sari did.

That winter, their family went skiing during the short pink hours of sunlight. The trees were covered in frost so thick they looked like glass sculptures.

Aleksi was fast — always racing ahead, fearless.
Sari was slower, but she liked to hum while she skied.
Music helped her feel brave.

Suddenly, the wind picked up. A gust of snow, a hidden drop.
A wrong turn.

Aleksi and Sari became separated.
And within minutes — the forest swallowed them both.

The mountain was silent again.

Aleksi shouted, but the snow took his voice.
Sari sat on a rock and cried.

And then... something strange happened.
She heard music.

Not from a phone. Not from the wind.

A melody — slow, rubato, rising and falling gently like breath.
Almost like her own humming, but older. Wiser.

Sari followed the sound. Not blindly — peacefully.
The snow stopped falling where she walked. The wind grew quiet.
She felt... warm.

At the same time, Aleksi saw a flicker of light between the trees. Not a flame — more like a shimmer. Like a snowflake that had remembered how to glow.

He followed.

And there, beneath a snow-laden pine, he found her.

Sari, safe. Humming. Smiling. Holding a tiny pinecone in her mitten like a gift.

When they were found by the search team an hour later, they said nothing about the music or the glowing snow.

But later, back in the cabin, Aleksi looked out the window and whispered:

"It's real, isn't it?"

Sari nodded.

"The mountain took care of us."

And sometimes, when the wind is soft and the snow drifts slow, you can still hear the Mountain Spirit — singing to those who need it most.

Let's explore music

Mood & Imagery

1. What kind of place does this piece make you imagine?
   A snowy mountain? A forest? A quiet cave?
   Describe what you "see" when you play or listen.
2. How would you describe the mood of this piece?
   (Lonely? Peaceful? Magical? Mysterious?)
3. Which part of the story does the music match most closely?
   Sari getting lost?
   The spirit appearing?
   The siblings reuniting?
4. If this piece had weather, what would it be?
   (Still snowfall? Cold wind? Sunlight on ice?)

Rubato, Repetition & Expression

5. What is rubato, and how does it work in this piece?
   Does the tempo stretch and pull like breathing?
   How does that make the music feel more alive?
6. There are many repeated phrases in this piece. Do they feel exactly the same each time?
   Or do they change slightly in volume, mood, or colour?
7. How would you shape a repeated melody, so it feels like it's telling a story — not just repeating itself?
8. Where in the music do you hear a "pause" — like a space for the spirit to appear or speak?
   How can you show that in your playing?

Harry and Ginny

Harry Potter and the Deathly Hallows Part I
by Alexandre Desplat

In a small Irish town with rainy rooftops and quiet streets, two eleven-year-olds named Harry and Ginny lived just three doors apart.

It was pure coincidence — their names.

They weren't related. They didn't go to Hogwarts.

But they were completely convinced they were meant to be a wizard and a witch.

Every day after school, they'd meet in the garden or under the old railway bridge to practise their "magic."
- Wands made from broom handles
- Spells written in glitter pen
- Potions made from grass clippings, orange soda, and toothpaste

Everyone laughed at them — including their teachers, their parents, and the mean kids at school.

"You're just playing dress-up," they'd say.
"Grow up."

But Harry and Ginny didn't stop.

One Saturday afternoon, they went into the woods behind the village — a wild place where the trees were tall, tangled, and dripping with green moss.

They brought a new spell Ginny had made up the night before, called "Phoenix Revealicus."

It was meant to bring them a sign.
A sign that magic was real.

They closed their eyes. Whispered the spell.

And when they opened them… something was there.

High in the trees, glowing like firelight on snow, perched a phoenix.

Its feathers shimmered gold and crimson. Its eyes sparkled like stars. And its voice was soft, low, and musical.

"You are not wrong," it said.

"But no one else needs to believe it for it to be true."

The phoenix hovered, its wings like stained glass in the sun.

"Keep creating. Keep imagining. And never stop chasing the kind of magic only you can see."

Then — like mist in morning light — it was gone.

Harry and Ginny stood still for a long time.

They didn't speak.

They didn't need to.

Because something had changed.

Not around them — but in them.

They kept doing magic.
Kept inventing.
And they never let the world laugh them out of believing again.

Because sometimes, the real magic…
is having the courage to believe in it — when no one else does.

Let's explore music

Mood & Emotion

1. What kind of mood does this piece create?
   (Mysterious? Sad? Magical? Hopeful?)
   How do you feel when you play or listen to it?
2. Which part of the story does this music remind you of most?
   The kids pretending to do spells?
   Being laughed at?
   Meeting the phoenix?
3. Does the music sound more like imagination... or reality?
   How can you show that difference in the way you play?
4. If this piece were a scene from a film, what would be happening on screen?

Melody, Harmony & Touch

5. Is the melody smooth (legato) or broken (staccato)?
   What kind of feeling does that create?
6. Do the harmonies sound calm or tense?
   Where in the music do you feel something is about to happen?
7. Can you play this piece as if you are telling a secret?
   How would that change your dynamics and touch?
8. Which note or phrase in the piece feels like a "spark" — the moment something magical happens?
   How would you bring that out?

Once Upon a December
by Lynn Ahrens & Stephen Flaherty
Russia, 1917.

The snow was falling quietly in Saint Petersburg, covering the grand palaces in silence. But inside the city, everything was loud — whispers of revolution, fear, and families preparing to run.

Fourteen-year-old Anastasia Ivanovna was the daughter of a cousin of Tsar Nicholas II. Her family lived in a fine house — not quite royal, but still too close to the throne for comfort.

Her father had always warned that hard times were coming. And now, those times had arrived.

One cold December night, a friend of the family arrived at the back door, breathless and pale.

"They're coming for you," he said.
"You must leave tonight."

There was no time to pack, no time for goodbyes.

Anastasia, her little brother Theodorov, and their parents dressed as poor villagers and slipped into the streets, walking quickly toward the station. Their hope: a train to Paris, where distant relatives might take them in.

But just before they reached the station, voices shouted behind them.

"Run," her father whispered.
"Don't wait. Just run."

Anastasia hesitated — just for a moment. Then she clutched the piece of paper with her uncle's Paris address, turned, and ran into the snow.

The station was full of smoke and shouting.

She had no money. No papers. No ticket.

But the train was there, steam hissing like breath on a window.

She climbed into the luggage car and hid beneath heavy coats, her heart pounding like a drum.

She didn't cry. She couldn't.

She watched the world vanish behind her, snow-covered and silent, as the train pulled away into the unknown.

Days later, she arrived in Paris — tired, frightened, alone.

She found her uncle's house. They took her in with tears and shock, never expecting to see her at all.

For a week, she said nothing.

She sat by the fire at night, watching the snow fall outside the window, remembering the sound of her mother's voice, her father's hands, her brother's laughter.

A life that felt like a dream.
And then, on the eighth day, someone knocked at the door.
It was them.

Her mother, pale and breathless.
Her father, eyes full of tears.
Little Theodorov, carrying a broken toy she thought was lost.

They had made it. All of them.

Their old world was gone. No more palaces, no more titles. But they had each other. And that was enough.

In the quiet of their new home, Anastasia would sometimes hum a lullaby her mother used to sing in Russia — soft, slow, full of snow and memory.

It began:
"Far away, long ago, glowing dim as an ember..."

And whenever December came again, she would remember that snowy night when she ran from her past and found her way into the future.

Let's explore music

Mood & Emotion

1. What mood does this piece create when you listen to or play it? (Nostalgic? Dreamy? Sad? Peaceful?)
2. Does the music sound like it is remembering something or telling a story in the present?
   What kind of memories might it be expressing?
3. Which part of the story matches the music best?
   Anastasia running alone?
   Her quiet arrival in Paris?
   The moment her family returns?
4. If you had to describe this music as a feeling, what would it be? (Hope? Longing? Love? Loss?)

Melody & Rubato

5. Is the melody smooth or angular? Legato or detached?
   How does this shape the story the music tells?
6. How does rubato (flexible tempo) help express emotion in this piece?
   Where might you slow down — like a memory lingering?
7. Are there parts that feel like a question... and parts that feel like an answer?
   How can you express that in your phrasing?
8. What makes the melody sound like it's "floating" or "drifting"? (Is it the rhythm? The phrasing? The key?)

Angry Birds
by Ari Pulkkinen

There was once a place so full of birdsong, it sounded like the sky itself was singing.

It was the Pantanal — a vast, shimmering land of rivers and trees in South America, where hundreds of bird species lived together in bright, beautiful harmony.

Parrots and toucans, herons and macaws — they built their nests in tall trees, taught their chicks to fly, and sang to the sun each morning like it was a friend.

It was a paradise of feathers and wings.

The birds weren't just neighbours.
They were a community.

- The older birds kept a watchful eye out for storms.
- The young ones brought twigs and berries to help build nests.
- The parents shared food and shaded their chicks with wide, gentle wings.

They had no leaders, no rules — only rhythm, cooperation, and song.

But one day, the sky went silent.

Not because of the weather.
Because of machines.

Humans had arrived — not with binoculars or notebooks, but with chainsaws and plans.

"This land is perfect," they said.
"We'll build hotels! Pools! Roads! A paradise for people!"

They saw trees. But not homes.
They heard birdsong. But not voices.

The machines began to roar.

The trees fell.

The nests broke.

The birds flew — not away, but into hiding. Watching. Waiting.

Then something happened.

A call echoed through the canopy. Short, sharp, rising like thunder.

It was a warning cry.

And then, from every corner of the sky, they came.

They were not running.
They were fighting.

Swarming, swooping, squawking — in flocks so fast and furious the workers dropped their tools and ran for cover.

- Parrots yanked the maps from their hands.
- Falcons stole their hard hats.
- Woodpeckers drummed alarms on steel beams.

Even the baby birds joined in — flapping and peeping and dive-bombing with all their might.

The people ran.

They didn't stop to pack.
They didn't look back.

And the machines?
Silent at last.

The trees stood still.

The birds rebuilt. Slowly. Together.

The nests were new, but the song was the same.

And now, when the sun rises over the Pantanal, you can still hear it:

Not just a melody…

But a message.

"We are not decorations.
We are not background music.
This land is ours, too."

Humans can always find another place.
But nature will always fight to keep its own.

Let's explore music

What kind of musical mood do you hear in this piece?
(Is it exciting, playful, defiant, chaotic?)

1. How would you describe the rhythm of this piece?
   Does it feel like something marching, flying, or chasing?
2. Can you imagine the birds preparing for their defence while playing this piece?
   Which part of the music sounds like their surprise attack?
3. Do any parts of the piece feel like "teamwork"?
   How can you show that in your dynamics or articulation?
4. What instruments do you think would match this story if a whole band played it?
   (Example: drums for panic, flutes for birdsong, etc.)
5. Where would you play louder or more sharply to sound like angry birds?
   What techniques would help your playing sound "fierce but fun"?
6. How is this piece different from a sad or peaceful one?
   What does that teach you about how music tells a story?
7. If you were to write a second piece called "The Birds Rebuild," how would it sound different? What musical ideas would you use?

Geographical & Environmental Questions – The Pantanal (South America)
Focus: biodiversity, habitats, conservation

1. Where is the Pantanal located?
   (Bonus: Can you find it on a map of South America?)
2. Why is the Pantanal so important for birds and other wildlife?
   What kinds of animals live there besides birds?
3. What kind of habitat is the Pantanal?
   (Rainforest, wetland, desert...?)

Dynamite (BTS)
by David Stewart & Jessica Agombar

In the bustling city of Busan, South Korea, where neon signs light the night and the air buzzes with energy, lived a 13-year-old boy named Min-jun. Busan was a city of contrasts — sandy beaches and towering skyscrapers, ancient temples and glowing shopping arcades. Min-jun loved it all, but what he loved most was music. Especially BTS.

Ever since he heard Dynamite on the radio, something had changed in him. He danced in his room. He sang in the shower. He watched every live performance and dreamed of one day seeing them in person.

So when BTS announced a concert in Seoul — their only show that year — Min-jun felt like his heart would explode.

But tickets were expensive, and his parents, who ran a tiny seafood stall near Jagalchi Market, couldn't afford even one. Still, Min-jun didn't give up.
He made flyers for local cafes. He ran errands for neighbours. He even helped a bakery decorate cakes on weekends.

That's when he met Hyun-woo, another boy his age who was also working part-time at the same bakery. At first, they barely spoke — until Hyun-woo caught Min-jun humming Dynamite while frosting cupcakes.

"You're a BTS fan too?" Hyun-woo grinned.

From that moment, they were a team. They practiced choreography in the park. They split jobs. They kept each other going when work got tough or money came in slowly.

Finally — one week before the concert — they had just enough.

The night of the concert, Seoul's Olympic Stadium sparkled with lights, cheers, and the heartbeat of thousands of fans. When Dynamite started playing, Min-jun and Hyun-woo jumped, shouted, danced — not as strangers or workers, but as friends who believed in dreams.

And for three magical hours, they didn't feel poor or tired.

They felt alive.

Because music — especially K-pop — has a way of making everything shine a little brighter. Like dynamite.

Let's explore music

1. What does K-pop stand for, and what makes it special compared to other styles of pop music?

2. "Dynamite" is known for its upbeat, danceable rhythm. What instruments or sounds can you hear that make it feel energetic and fun?

3. How does music like "Dynamite" affect your mood when you listen or dance to it? Can music give you more energy or happiness?

4. The song uses a strong beat and catchy melody. What do you think makes a melody "catchy"? Can you hum part of the chorus?

5. In the story, Min-jun and Hyun-woo bond over music. Can you think of a time music helped you connect with someone?

6. Why do you think K-pop includes choreography as part of its performance? How does dance change the way you experience a song?

7. If you were to choreograph a small routine to a song like "Dynamite," what kinds of movements would you include — fast, slow, sharp, smooth? Why?

8. How does this song reflect modern pop music — and what makes it different from classical or traditional songs you've learned before?
9. Can you find the tempo of "Dynamite"? Would you describe it as slow, moderate, or fast?

Chord Etude
by Ray Moore

In the red-dusted hills of the Northern Territory, far from the big cities of Australia, lived a girl named Kirra. Her family were part of the Arrernte people, and the sound of the wind, birds, and ancestral songs filled her days.

Kirra was only nine, but she had a quiet fire in her heart — and a big dream. She wanted to play the piano.

Her school had one old upright piano, kept in a corner of the hall and rarely tuned. Still, every day after class, Kirra would stay behind and practise with her teacher, Miss Lisa.

There was just one problem: chords.

Kirra had small hands, and when Miss Lisa first showed her a chord with four or five notes, her fingers just wouldn't reach.

"It's okay," Miss Lisa said gently. "You don't have to stretch all at once. You can break the chord — one note at a time. That's still music."

But Kirra wanted to do more than break chords. She wanted to feel them ringing under her fingers like thunder across the desert.

So she practised. Slowly, patiently.
She learned to roll her wrist, to position her hand just right, and to use the weight of her arm — not just the strength of her fingers.

Weeks turned to months. And one day, she played a chord with a flat 13th — cleanly, with confidence.

It sounded... beautiful.
A little mysterious. A little jazzy.
Full of colours she had never heard before.

Inspired, Kirra began making her own little songs — simple at first, but full of rich harmonies. Chords were no longer her enemy. They were her language.

She called her first composition Desert Rain and played it for her class during assembly.

Nobody spoke while she played. The piano, once forgotten, sang with bold, colourful chords that echoed like clouds bursting over the plains.

When she finished, everyone clapped. Her hands were still small — but her sound was big.
Kirra smiled and whispered to herself:
"Even small hands can make big music."

Let's explore music

1. What is a chord?
    Can you name some chords you already know?
2. The piece uses colourful harmonies, including 7ths and 9ths.
    Can you play a C major chord and then turn it into a C7? What does it sound like?
3. What is a flat 13th chord?
    Try playing one with your teacher. How does it sound compared to a regular major chord?
4. What does the word "etude" mean?
    Why do you think this piece is called a "Chord Etude"?
5. In the story, Kirra had trouble with wide chords.
    What techniques can pianists use if they have small hands?
6. How do chords help create emotion in music?
    Think of a major chord and a minor chord. What's the emotional difference?
7. Can you create a short melody using only chords?
    Try making a 3-chord progression and playing it with different rhythms.

Geographical Questions

1. Where is Australia located on the world map?
   Is it in the Northern or Southern Hemisphere?

2. Who are the Aboriginal peoples of Australia?
   Can you name any traditional Aboriginal instruments?

3. What is the climate like in the Australian outback or bush?
   How might living in that environment affect someone's daily life or music practice?

4. What are some famous cities in Australia where people go to learn or perform music?
   (e.g., Sydney, Melbourne — can you find them on a map?)

All Blues or "Blue Notes at Midnight"

by Miles Davis

New York City, 1945

In the cold winter of 1945, Nathaniel Green, a 17-year-old trumpet prodigy from Chicago, stepped off the train at Grand Central Station with a worn-out suitcase and a shiny brass trumpet wrapped in an old scarf.

He had just been accepted into the Juilliard School of Music — the dream of every serious musician in America.
The war had just ended. New York was buzzing with jazz clubs, GIs coming home, and music pouring out of every radio and rooftop.

But Juilliard wasn't easy.

Nathaniel practiced twelve hours a day — scales, études, classical pieces. He shared a tiny room with two other students, ate cold sandwiches for dinner, and missed his family terribly.

One night, walking home past Minton's Playhouse in Harlem, he heard something that stopped him cold.
A trumpet — smoother than velvet, darker than the city sky.
He leaned in and saw a man on stage playing jazz as if it were breathing.

It was Miles Davis, still young but already a legend in the making.

Nathaniel returned night after night.
Eventually, Miles noticed.
"Juilliard kid?" he asked one evening.
Nathaniel nodded, speechless.
Miles handed him a trumpet.
"Let's see if you got soul in your fingers."

From that night on, Nathaniel lived in two worlds — the strict discipline of Juilliard by day... and the smoky, swing-filled freedom of Harlem's jazz scene by night.

He learned that music wasn't just notes on a page — it was feeling. It was sorrow, joy, rebellion, and hope.

Years later, people would say Nathaniel's sound reminded them of All Blues — not because he copied it...
but because he had learned what it meant to feel the blues.

Let's explore music

1. What is jazz and how is it different from classical music?

2. What is a blues scale and how does it sound compared to a major scale?

3. What instrument did Miles Davis play, and what makes the trumpet special in jazz?

4. What does improvisation mean in music, and why is it so important in jazz?

5. In the story, Nathaniel learns that music is more than technique. Can you explain what this means?

6. What is a blue note, and how might it make a piece of music feel?

7. Why do you think "All Blues" is considered a timeless piece of jazz music?

Geographical & Historical Questions (1940s New York & Jazz Culture)

1. What was the Juilliard School, and why was it important in American music history?

2. Where is Harlem, and what role did it play in the history of jazz?

3. What major historical event had just ended in 1945, and how did that affect life in cities like New York?

4. Why do you think jazz clubs like Minton's Playhouse were so important for young musicians in the 1940s?

Tres Palabras
by Osvaldo Farres

Cuba, 1956

In the lush green fields of Vinales, where tobacco leaves stretch under the Caribbean sun and mountains hug the sky, lived a 14-year-old girl named Luz Maria. She worked in the fields with her parents and brothers, rising at dawn and returning with sun-kissed skin and calloused hands.

But each evening, after her chores, Luz would walk to the sea. The beach was her escape — a quiet place where the breeze played with her curls and the waves hummed lullabies. She often dreamt of a life beyond the fields, filled with music, colours, and friends.

One golden evening, while strolling barefoot along the shore, Luz saw something glimmering in the sand. It was a strange oyster, large and luminous, with shades of violet and silver. As she picked it up, it opened on its own, and from inside came a soft, echoing voice:

"Say three words — not sentences, just words. Three words from the heart. And your wish will unfold."

Luz blinked. Was she imagining this? But the voice sounded kind... and real.

She held the oyster to her chest and whispered:
"Musica. Baile. Amigos."(MCsic. Dance. Friends.)

The wind picked up. The waves shimmered. Suddenly, in front of her eyes, the beach transformed.

Torches lit up along the shore. A band of drummers began to play infectious Cuban rhythms. Young people her age appeared, laughing, singing, dancing barefoot on the sand. Someone handed Luz a maraca. Another pulled her into a circle of dancers.

She had never felt such joy.

It was as if all her dreams had taken shape — a world where rhythm ruled, friendships were born in a heartbeat, and music spoke louder than words.

As the night deepened, the oyster glowed faintly in her pocket, as if smiling.

From that day forward, every evening after work, Luz would visit the beach. The magical music never left her heart. And even when she became a music teacher years later, she always told her students:

"Sometimes, all it takes is three words... said with truth."

Let's explore music

1. What does "Tres Palabras" mean in Spanish? What could these three words represent in music or life?

2. Cuban music often features percussion instruments. Can you name some Cuban or Latin instruments that might be heard in this story's beach celebration? (e.g., bongos, maracas, claves, congas)

3. How does music create a mood or bring people together, like in the story? Can you describe a time when music made you feel connected or happy?

4. In the story, Luz says three words: "Música, Baile, Amigos." How can music, dance, and friendship work together in real life?

5. What rhythms or styles are often used in Cuban music? Have you heard any music that makes you want to dance? (Salsa, Son Cubano, Cha-cha-cha, Rumba)

Geographical & Cultural Questions:

1. Where is Cuba located on the map? What kind of climate and nature do you think it has, based on the story?

2. What are some famous Cuban cultural traditions, especially related to music and dance?

3. Why do you think music is so important in Cuban daily life, especially for young people like Luz?

4. Do you know any Cuban musicians or songs? Can you compare Cuban music to music from your own country?

5. If you could choose three words to shape a magical world like Luz's, what would your three words be — and why?

The End

Printed in Dunstable, United Kingdom